Editor: Penny Clarke
Artists: Mark Bergin
          Nick Hewetson

Produced by
THE SALARIYA BOOK CO. LTD
25 Marlborough Place
Brighton BN1 5UB

Published by
PETER BEDRICK BOOKS
2112 Broadway
New York, NY 10023

Library of Congress Cataloging-in-Publication
Data

Macdonald, Fiona.
     First facts about the ancient Greeks /
     written by Fiona Macdonald; created &
     designed by David Salariya.
        p. cm. — (The first facts series)
     Includes index.
     Summary: Surveys the food, hairstyles,
jewelry, religion, festivals, sports, science,
warfare, and other aspects of life in ancient
Greece.
     ISBN 0-87226-532-3
     1. Greece—Civilization—To 146 B.C.—
Juvenile literature. 2. Greece—Social life and
customs—Pictorial works—Juvenile literature.
[1. Greece—Civilization—To 146 B.C.]
I. Salariya, David.   II. Title.   III. Series: First
facts (Peter Bedrick Books)
DF77.M163   1997
938—dc21   97-7209
                                   CIP
                                   AC

5 4 3 2 1 98 99 00 01 02 03 04 05
Printed in Hong Kong.

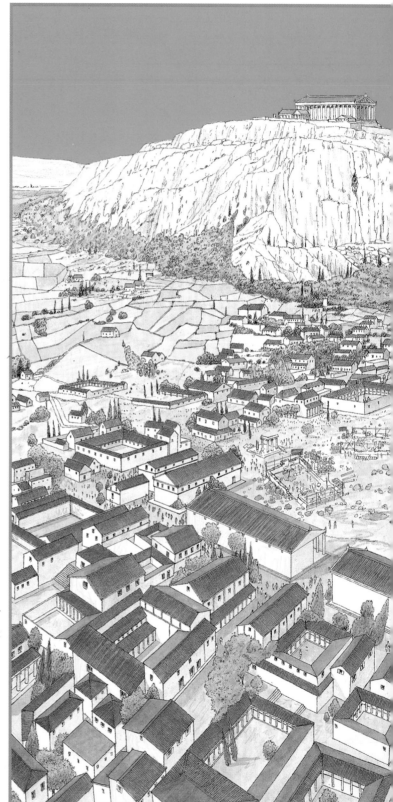

FIRST FACTS
about the
ANCIENT
GREEKS

Written by
FIONA MACDONALD

Created & Designed by
DAVID SALARIYA

PETER BEDRICK BOOKS

ONTENTS

7 INTRODUCTION

8 FACT: MANY GREEKS LIVED FAR FROM HOME

10 FACT: THE GREEKS INVENTED DEMOCRACY

12 FACT: GREEKS ACTORS WORE MASKS ONSTAGE

14 FACT: THE GREEKS IMPORTED FLOUR FROM EGYPT

16 FACT: MARRIED WOMEN STAYED HOME

18 FACT: GREEK CLOTHES NEEDED NO SEWING

20 FACT: GREEKS BUILT HOUSES FOR THE GODS

22 FACT: GREEKS SACRIFICED ANIMALS TO THE GODS

24 FACT: ATHLETES RACED IN THE NUDE

26 FACT: DOCTORS SWORE A SOLEMN OATH

28 FACT: SOLDIERS HUNG THEIR ARMOR IN TREES

30 GLOSSARY

31 INDEX

INTRODUCTION

THE ANCIENT GREEKS lived over 2,500 years ago – Greek civilization flourished from around 800 to 300 BC. It was a time of great achievements: Greek architects designed marvelous buildings, Greek potters, painters and sculptors created beautiful works of art, and Greek writers composed poems and plays that are still enjoyed today. Greek scientists and scholars made many new discoveries, especially in math and medicine; Greek philosophers investigated how our minds work and debated important questions, such as, 'What is the right way to live?' Greek politicians developed new ways of running their city-states, and gave ordinary people a part in the government.

In spite of all these achievements, the Greeks faced serious problems, too. The Greek population was growing, some areas, particularly the islands, were overcrowded, and frequently suffered shortages of food. There were also epidemics of deadly disease. Between 430 and 429 BC some 75,000 people died of the plague in Athens – about a quarter of the population.

Greek city-states were rivals and were often at war with each other. The Greeks also faced attack by enemies from overseas. The Persians invaded twice: in 490 and 480 BC, but the city-states formed alliances and their armies forced the Persians to retreat. However, after King Philip of Macedon (the father of Alexander the Great) conquered Greece in 338 BC, Greek power finally began to decline.

FACT: MANY GREEKS LIVED FAR FROM HOME

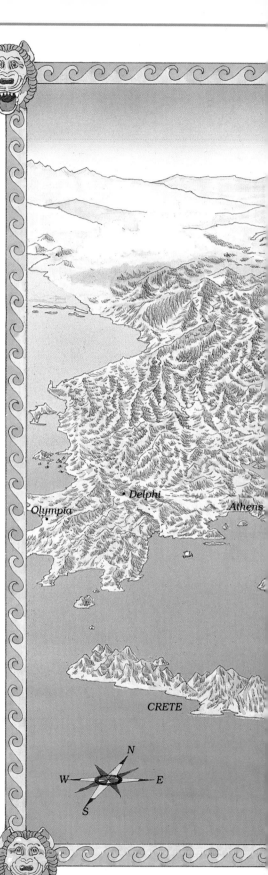

THE ANCIENT GREEKS' homeland included mainland Greece, hundreds of islands in the Mediterranean Sea, and settlements all along the coast of western Turkey.

The landscape of these Greek homelands was rugged and very beautiful, with high, snow-capped mountains, shady valleys and steep, jagged cliffs sweeping down to the seashore. But, especially on the islands, there was very little flat land or good, rich soil suitable for growing crops.

Over the centuries the Greek population increased rapidly, and by about 750 BC, many families were forced by hunger to leave their homes and seek a new life overseas. They set up colonies, which they organized and governed like their towns and villages back home. These colonies remained loyal allies of Greece for centuries, in peacetime and in war.

Greek settlers also took their own civilization with them wherever they went. Greek words, ideas and artistic styles spread to many other Mediterranean lands. Their influence has lasted for thousands of years.

Facts about the Greeks' Language:

Poetry and plays written in the Greek language were an important part of Greek culture. To record them, Greek scribes devised an alphabet based on an earlier one invented by the Phoenicians.

We still use the Greek alphabet, in a modernized form. And many Greek words, from 'mega' (big) to 'micro' (minute), are used in languages throughout the world.

FAMILIES from the Greek mainland and islands settled in Sicily, southern France and on the west coast of Turkey. Greek traders made long sea voyages to trade in distant lands, from Phoenicia and Egypt in the east to Carthage in the west.

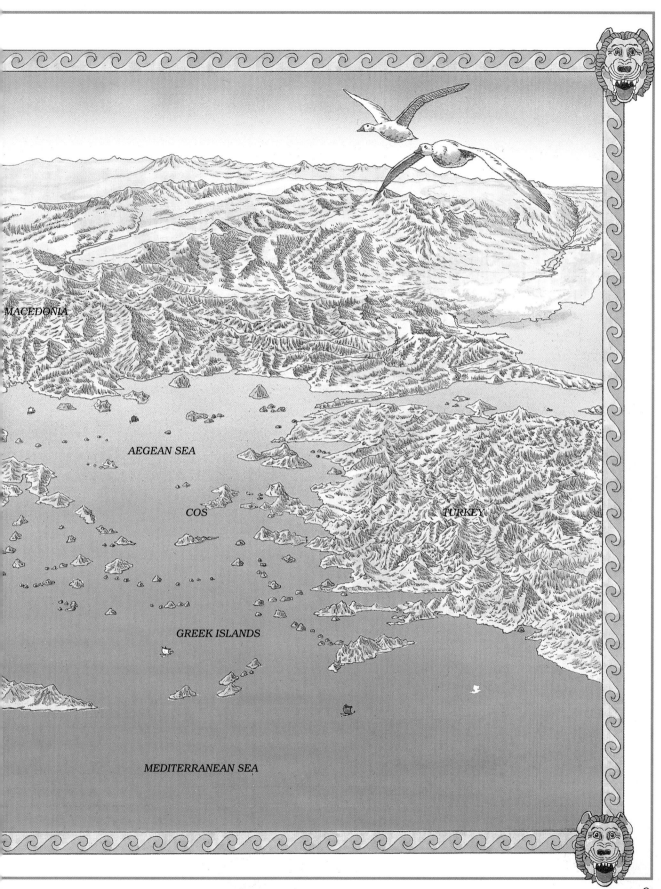

MACEDONIA

AEGEAN SEA

COS

TURKEY

GREEK ISLANDS

MEDITERRANEAN SEA

9

FACT: THE GREEKS INVENTED DEMOCRACY

THE GREEK homelands were divided into small, self-governing city-states. Each consisted of a city or large town and the countryside around it. Each one chose its own leaders, ran its own army and made its own laws. Athens was the largest and most powerful. Other city-states had only a few thousand citizens.

The first city-states were ruled by kings. Then 'tyrants' (strong men) or 'oligarchs' (rich men) seized power. Around 500 BC, a new form of government developed: 'democracy', rule by the people.

In Athens all important decisions were made by the Assembly of citizens. Members could make speeches and vote on government policy. They could also vote to 'ostracize' (expel) unpopular politicians. Ostracized people had to leave Athens for at least 10 years.

Facts about Government:

If too few citizens came to a meeting of the Athenian Assembly, the city police force had to go and round up some more.

Citizens could not speak for too long in Assembly debates. They were timed by a water-clock. When the water ran out, they had to stop speaking and sit down.

JURIES used ballot tokens to show their verdict: a token with a solid central lug meant 'innocent', one with a hollow lug meant 'guilty'.

MEMBERS of a jury casting their bronze ballot tokens into the jar. When every one had voted, the jar was emptied and the number of guilty and innocent tokens counted.

EVERY YEAR, 500 citizens of Athens were chosen to be members of the city Council. They planned new laws and proposed new policies, then the assembly debated them. Fifty Council members took it in turns to be on duty, day and night, so no one person could make a major decision.

DEMOCRATIC government was introduced in Athens in 508 BC. All free men were entitled to vote. Women were not.

THE ASSEMBLY, which made all main government decisions, met every 10 days. At least 6,000 citizens had to attend.

FACT: GREEK ACTORS WORE MASKS ONSTAGE

THE GREEKS enjoyed singing, dancing, listening to music and going to the theatre. Musicians and dancers entertained guests at dinner parties, and performed at weddings and funerals. Religious festivals, sports events and military parades included singing and dancing. Plays were the most popular entertainments. They often had a 'message', praising or criticizing political leaders, or debating controversial topics. Most cities had an open-air theatre – the largest held about 10,000 people. Slaves were not allowed to go.

MASKS for comic parts in plays had laughing expressions. Masks for tragic plays were sad and sorrowful.

Facts about Greek Theatre:

All Greek actors were men. They wore masks with exaggerated expressions, so that people sitting at the back of the theatre could see them. To play women's roles, actors wore wigs and padded clothes.

Pregnant women were banned from some dramatic plays in case the violence on stage upset them and caused a miscarriage.

THE TOWN'S AGORA (market-place) provided its own form of entertainment. Men met their friends, talked politics and admired the goods on sale, among them luxuries imported from the Middle East.

FACT: THE GREEKS IMPORTED FLOUR FROM EGYPT

GREEK FARMERS had to work hard to make a living. Their land was stony and the climate harsh. Few crops flourished in Greek soil – only barley, lentils and sesame seeds. To make good quality bread, the Greeks imported wheat from Egypt, far away across the Mediterranean Sea.

However, grapevines and olive trees grew very well. As a result, some farmers did not clear fields or plow the land, but devoted most of their farms to these crops. Grapes were dried in the hot summer sun to make raisins, or crushed and fermented to make wine. Olives were pickled in salty water, to preserve them, or pressed to make olive oil.

On the wild, steep mountain slopes, farmers kept flocks of sheep and herds of goats to provide milk and meat for food, skins for leather, and wool or hair to spin and weave to make cloth.

Rich farmers had slaves and servants to do the work. Poor farmers had only their wives and children to help them.

THE GREEKS' diet was very healthy, with lots of bread, beans and olives. In the summer, there were vegetables, fresh fruit and herbs, and in winter, apples, chestnuts, lentils and cheese. The Greeks did not have sugar, but used flower-scented honey instead. The sea provided much of their food. Squid, sea urchins, octopus and fish were all popular.

OLIVE OIL was so valuable that it was given as prizes to winners in the Olympic Games.

RICH MEN invited their friends to dinner parties, called symposia. The host and his guests reclined on couches, while slaves served them with food and wine. Women were rarely guests at such parties. Although often intended as occasions for serious conversation, symposia were sometimes just an excuse for a drinking party.

Facts about Ancient Greek Food and Diet:

Respectable women didn't go shopping. Instead, they sent their husbands or servants to the market.

The Greeks admired slim, athletic figures. Being fat or flabby was seen as a sign of self-indulgence.

Food was used as a weapon in war. When enemy troops besieged a city, they would poison the water supply and set fire to crops in the fields around it.

Men hunted hare and deer, while women gathered herbs, mushrooms and berries.

OLIVE OIL was made by crushing ripe green olives between heavy stones, using a huge wooden lever to work the olive press. Top-quality oil was used for cooking and to preserve food. Lower-grade oil was burned in lamps, or used to clean and soften the skin.

FINE drinking cups, often shaped like an animal's head, were used by rich families. Poor people used plain clay mugs.

GREEK WIVES and daughters usually did the cooking, but rich families employed cooks to prepare feasts.

WHETHER they were rich or poor, the Greeks always drank their wine mixed with water. They mixed the wine and water in big pottery jars like the two in the picture (left).

FACT: MARRIED WOMEN STAYED AT HOME

GREEK TOWNS were often busy, noisy and dirty. The narrow streets were crowded with people running errands and messengers hurrying around. There was hammering from craft workshops, shouting, and the clatter of horses' hooves. There were no sewers, so drains and trash heaps gave off a horrible smell. At night, towns could be dangerous. Thieves lurked in dark alleyways, ready to attack unsuspecting passers-by on their way home.

For all these reasons, it was neither safe nor pleasant for women to walk through city streets alone. It was also not considered 'respectable'. Women and girls from noble or wealthy families were not supposed to meet men from outside their own family, or to appear in public without an escort or a veil to hide their face. Many women spent most of their lives at home. They were busy running the household and organizing the servants. Some took private lessons, becoming scholars or musicians.

Facts about Families:

When a woman got married, she was carried in a torchlight procession to her husband's house. There, she had to learn to get along on with all his family. Several generations of a family usually shared the same home.

Greek parents loved their children, but brought them up strictly. Children were taught to be hard-working and obedient, and to respect older people.

TOWNHOUSES like this were the homes of prosperous craftworkers and their families. It is planned around a central courtyard, and has high walls and a strong gate for security. There is a workshop and rooms for cooking, sleeping and entertaining.

STOREROOMS were used to keep stocks of oil, wine, dried fruit and vegetables for the winter. They were also used to store finished goods, ready for sale.

storeroom

MEALS were cooked in the courtyard, over an open fire.

THERE WAS a separate room for women where wives, daughters and female slaves spun thread and wove cloth.

WALLS were made of sun-dried mud bricks or plastered stone. Roofs were made of baked clay tiles.

THE FAMILY'S bedrooms were upstairs and furnished with carved wooden beds, chairs and storage chests.

THERE WAS a room where slaves ate and slept. Many craftsmen owned slaves. They also employed trained assistants to help them.

slaves' rooms

family's sitting room

THE FAMILY could relax together in the private sitting room, where they also ate their meals. On special occasions it was also used for dinner parties, but these were strictly for men only.

altar for family prayers

inner courtyard

17

FACT: GREEK CLOTHES NEEDED NO SEWING

GREEK CLOTHES were simple – but very elegant. Graceful styles could easily be created without the need for sewing by folding long lengths of fabric and holding them in place with brooches or little metal clasps.

Men's and women's clothes were similar in design. Men and women both wore a simple tunic, called a 'chiton', and a long cloak, or 'himation'. Women often wore a shorter, decorated tunic, called a 'peplos' over their chiton. For work, men sometimes wore just a loincloth. Everyone went barefoot, or wore simple leather sandals. Wealthy women liked gold and silver jewelry, and employed slaves to arrange their hair in the elaborate styles that were fashionable.

Facts about Fashion:
Poor people could only afford rough, undyed wool cloth, in shades of cream or brown. The wealthy liked brightly colored robes. Purple cloth was the most expensive.

Pale complexions were the fashion for women – only slaves or servants who worked outside had a tan. It was fashionable to use make-up made from mineral pigments and berry juices.

Soldiers from Sparta grew their hair until it hung in curls down their backs. They combed it carefully before battle.

IN SUMMER peasants wore a loincloth and a straw hat. In winter, they wore woolen tunics, a leather hat and boots. A cloak was useful on a journey.

FIBULAE (brooches) were used to fasten clothes at the shoulder.

THIS SERVANT wears a long chiton with a short peplos on top.

MORE ELABORATE dresses were fastened with small metal clasps.

HISTORIANS AND ARCHAEOLOGISTS have learned a great deal about Greek clothes from carvings on tombstones. Clothes like this were worn around 400 BC.

AROUND 450 BC, Greek clothes were often decorated with borders in this 'Greek Key' pattern (above). The Greeks called the design a 'meander' after the winding River Meander in Turkey.

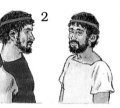

GREEK HAIRSTYLES changed over the centuries.
1 Before about 600 BC, men and women wore long hair and head-bands.
2 From about 500 BC, men's hair and beards were shorter and women wore their hair up.
3 After about 350 BC, men had very short hair and no beards. Fashionable women had curls.

GREEK JEWELRY:
1 Gold clasp for fastening fine clothes.
2 Gold necklace, made c.450 BC.
3 Gold earrings, made c.350 BC.
4 Ring shaped like a snake.

TO GIVE their clothes shape, women wore a girdle around the waist.

WORKING men wore short tunics, sandals and a cloak.

WOMEN wore long cloaks over their floor-length chitons.

OLDER MEN often wore long chitons over full-length tunics.

FACT: THE GREEKS BUILT HOUSES FOR THE GODS

GREEK TEMPLES were built as homes for gods and goddesses, whose spirits, the Greeks believed, lived in or visited the temples. So they used the best architects and craftsmen to build temples at ancient holy sites. The earliest Greek temples, built around 900 BC, were simple wooden shelters. Later temples were built of stone, which was more difficult to work with, and also more expensive. The basic design remained the same, but stone columns held up the roof instead of tree trunks.

Temples also showed the wealth and power of a city-state. The richest, like Athens, built temples of fine materials, such as sparkling white marble, and decorated them with statues, paintings and carvings.

THE ACROPOLIS at Athens was a fortress and a holy place. Its temples were magnificently rebuilt in the 5th century BC, when the city was at the height of its power.

SUPERB statues, many more than life-size, decorate the front of the Parthenon, the principal temple, on the Acropolis. Inside, there was a statue to the goddess Athene that was over 30 feet high and made of pure ivory and gold.

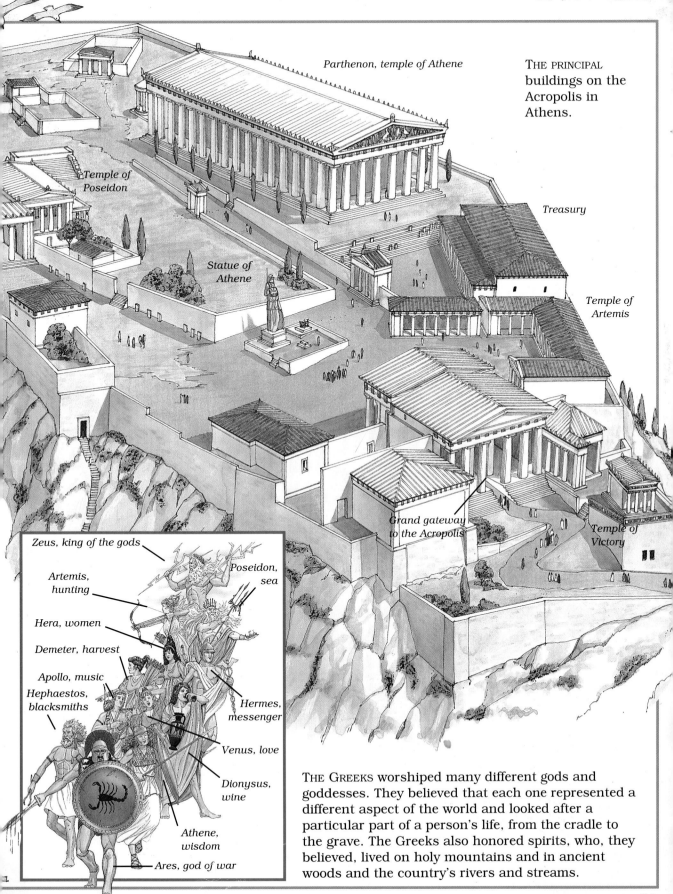

Parthenon, temple of Athene

THE PRINCIPAL buildings on the Acropolis in Athens.

Temple of Poseidon

Treasury

Statue of Athene

Temple of Artemis

Grand gateway to the Acropolis

Temple of Victory

Zeus, king of the gods

Artemis, hunting

Poseidon, sea

Hera, women

Demeter, harvest

Apollo, music

Hephaestos, blacksmiths

Hermes, messenger

Venus, love

Dionysus, wine

Athene, wisdom

Ares, god of war

THE GREEKS worshiped many different gods and goddesses. They believed that each one represented a different aspect of the world and looked after a particular part of a person's life, from the cradle to the grave. The Greeks also honored spirits, who, they believed, lived on holy mountains and in ancient woods and the country's rivers and streams.

FACT: GREEKS SACRIFICED ANIMALS TO THE GODS

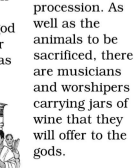

SACRIFICES took place at altars built outside temples. This vase-painting shows two priests about to sacrifice an animal by cutting its throat. Afterwards, they would burn the skin and bones of the slaughtered animal on the altar.

BEFORE an important sacrifice priests led a procession (below) to the temple of the god in whose honor the sacrifice was to be made.

CARVED STONE frieze of a festival procession. As well as the animals to be sacrificed, there are musicians and worshipers carrying jars of wine that they will offer to the gods.

ONLY the finest animals were worthy of sacrifice to the gods. They were washed and garlanded with flowers before being sacrificed.

RELIGIOUS FESTIVALS were important in many Greek cities. Festivals were held at regular intervals during the year, to honor the many different gods and goddesses, and sometimes ancient local heroes, too. Festival days were holidays, when few people worked. Instead, they took part in processions to the temples, or sang and danced in the streets. Some festivals were for separate groups in the community, such as farmers, or athletes, or women and young girls. Some were very mysterious, involving secret night-time rituals in caves deep underground. Women worshipers of Dionysus, the god of wine, sometimes ran wild in a drunken frenzy. Critics accused them of trampling crops as they staggered across the countryside at night.

Most festivals involved offering sacrifices to the gods, of fine animals, wine or special foods. The Greeks believed that if they gave presents to the gods, then the gods would help or protect them in return.

VASE-PAINTING showing a priestess tending an altar fire, while a priest sprinkles drops of wine on the flames. The Greeks believed that smoke from the fire would carry the sacrifice up to the gods in heaven.

SHARING FOOD was an important part of religion. After a sacrifice had been made, temple priests and their servants distributed the meat from the sacrifice. They also gave other offerings, such as wine, honey and barley cakes, to citizens who had taken part in the festival procession, or who had come to the temple to watch and pray. Sometimes these festival feasts went on all night.

Facts about Festivals:

The Panathenaia, the main festival in Athens, was held every four years to honor Athene, the city's own goddess. People marched to her temple on the Acropolis with a new robe for the huge statue of the goddess.

Rich men competed for the honor of providing a sacrifice at a festival.

FACT: ATHLETES RACED IN THE NUDE

GREEK MEN frequently went naked. For many months of the year the weather was very hot, so wearing no clothes made sense — even for battle-training, taking part in sports or for working in hot places like potteries or blacksmiths' forges. Greek men also admired beautiful bodies from an artistic point of view. However, women, except from dancers, were expected to be 'decently' covered all the time.

Sports festivals were held in many Greek city-states. The Olympic Games, held for five days every four years, were the most famous. According to legend, the first was in 776 BC, to honor Zeus, king of the gods. Winners were given a laurel-leaf crown (a sign of royalty) and many prizes. They were treated as heroes in their home towns and villages.

MANY SPORTS originated as fitness training for war. At the Olympics one race continued this tradition. Competitors had to race wearing a heavy metal war-helmet and carrying a big wooden shield. This made the race an extra test of stamina and strength.

WOMEN could not join in the men's games. Instead, they held their own at Olympia in years when the men's games were not held.

CHARIOT RACING was an exciting but dangerous sport. The charioteers drove light chariots, pulled by four horses.

OLYMPIA was a vast complex. It contained Zeus's temple, sports tracks, a stadium and a camp-site where visitors could stay.

FACTS

The 200 meter sprint was the most prestigious event for athletes to win. The racetrack at Olympia was 200 meters long (218 yards) and 30 meters (33 yards) wide. It was surfaced in white sand. The starting line was made of stone.

Referees at the Olympic Games kept order with a big stick.

FACT: DOCTORS SWORE A SOLEMN OATH

IN THE 5TH CENTURY BC, a Greek doctor called Hippocrates set up a training school for medical students on the Mediterranean island of Cos. He taught them all the latest medical knowledge, including anatomy and the use of drugs, and he also trained them to work in a strictly professional way. Student doctors had to swear an oath to live 'pure and holy lives', and to promise always to put the welfare of their patients first. The rules for good medical practice that Hippocrates laid down are still used today.

Greek scholars made scientific discoveries in many other fields beside medicine. Greek mathematicians discovered rules about numbers and shapes. Greek inventors designed water-clocks (one of which was used in the Athenian Assembly to stop people speaking too long in debates), automatic doors and the world's first slot machines. Greek geographers were among the first to calculate that the world was round.

APOLLO'S TEMPLE at Delphi (right) was home to an Oracle. People believed it could see into the future and came from all over Greece to ask its advice.

SOME GREEKS believed in faith-healing. They would go to the temple of Asclepius, the god of health and healing, where they would spend the night on the floor, close to the statue of the god. They hoped that during the night he would visit them in a dream and make them well again, or at least send them a dream that would reveal a cure for their illness.

GREEK SURGICAL instruments included spoons, tweezers, probes, spatulas and saws.

PATIENTS who were cured made the gods an offering shaped liked the part of their body that had been healed. Priests hung these on the temple's walls.

A DOCTOR examines his patient. Besides observing the patient's symptoms, Greek doctors were trained to study their lifestyle and emotional state as well.

GOVERNMENTS also consulted the Oracle. They believed it could help them make important decisions.

THE ORACLE spoke through a woman drugged by the smoke of burning laurel leaves. Priests asked her questions, then interpreted her answers.

Facts about Greek Science:

Archimedes, a Greek engineer, designed a machine (called the Archimedian screw) to make water flow uphill. His design remained in use for almost 2,000 years.

Greek doctors were probably the first to realize that our health can be affected by the environment. They studied the soil and water in regions where people often fell ill.

The Greek mathematician Pythagoras invented a new religion, based on the worship of numbers.

FACT: SOLDIERS HUNG THEIR ARMOR IN TREES

GREEK CITY-STATES were frequently at war, often with each other, but sometimes they formed an alliance to defend their homeland against foreign enemies. All men were supposed to serve in the army, joining at 18 as 'ephebes', or trainees, and serving for about two years.

Officers rode in war-chariots, and some city-states had cavalry, but most battles were fought on foot. The soldiers marched as a 'phalanx' (shoulder-to-shoulder) towards the enemy, presenting a wall of shields. At first, they attacked by hurling bronze-tipped spears, then they slashed and stabbed at the enemy with iron swords and daggers.

Facts about Wars:

Triremes, the biggest Greek warships, had crews of 170 oarsmen. They rowed in time to music played on a flute.

Soldiers who wanted to thank the gods for surviving a particularly bloody battle hung their armor in trees close to the battlefield.

In Sparta, a city-state in southern Greece, all the citizens were trained for war. Boys were taken from home at 7 years old, and taught to be tough, brave and obedient. Girls had to take part in lots of sports, so they would grow up to have strong, healthy children.

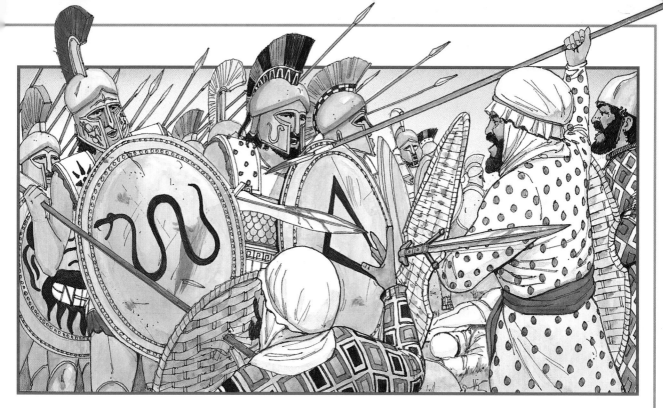

THE GREEKS AND PERSIANS were neighbors – and bitter enemies. The Persians invaded Greece in 490 BC and again in 480 BC. After several fierce battles the Greeks won. The Persians fought with bows and arrows, spears and daggers. They carried large shields of woven twigs and wore bright tunics and headgear.

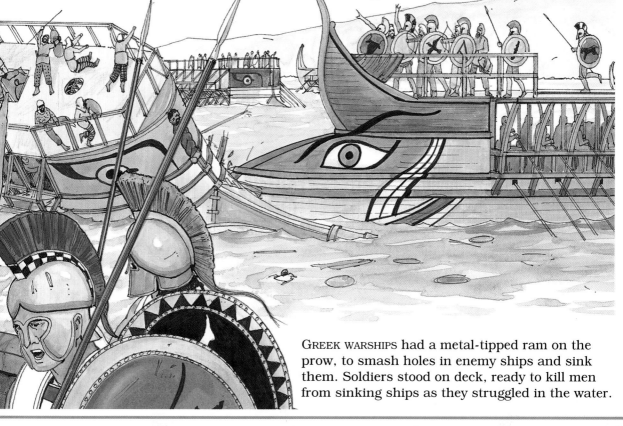

GREEK WARSHIPS had a metal-tipped ram on the prow, to smash holes in enemy ships and sink them. Soldiers stood on deck, ready to kill men from sinking ships as they struggled in the water.

Glossary

Acropolis ('high city') Fortress built on the highest part of a town. Important temples were often built there.

Altar Stone table outside Greek temples, where sacrifices to the gods were made.

Ancient Greeks People who lived in mainland Greece, the Greek islands and the west coast of Turkey from around 900 to 300 BC.

Ballot Small clay or metal token (about the size of a pebble) used by members of Athenian juries when indicating their verdicts.

Chiton Loose, flowing tunic. Men usually wore short ones, women's were always long.

Citizen Adult male who lived in a Greek city-state and who had rights, such as attending Assemblies where political decisions were made. Women, slaves and foreigners did not have these rights.

City-state City and the surrounding area with its own government.

Democracy Government by the people.

Himation Long cloak, worn by men and women.

Oligarchy Government by a small group of rich or powerful people. No one else had a say in the government of the state.

Oracle Place where the ancient Greeks believed they could learn the future by receiving a message from the gods.

Peplos Women's over-tunic.

Phoenicians People who lived in modern Lebanon and neighboring lands, from around 1100 to 300 BC.

Sacrifice Animals or special food offered to the gods in the hope of winning their help.

Shrine Holy site, where gods and spirits were worshiped.

Symposium (plural symposia) Dinner party for men only. Sometimes held for serious discussions, sometimes for drunken entertainment.

Tyrant Strong, dominant man, who took sole control of a city-state. He could govern as he liked, because there was nothing to check his power.

INDEX

A
Acropolis 20, 21, 23
actors 12, 13
agora 13
alphabet 8
Apollo 26
Archimedes 27
armor 28
army 7, 10, 28
Asclepius 26
Athene 20, 21, 23
Athens 10, 11, 20, 21, 23
    Assembly 10, 11, 26
    council 11
athletes 24, 25

B
ballot tokens 11
barley 14
    cakes 23
battles 18, 24, 28, 29
beans 14
beards 19
boys 28
bread 14

C
Carthage 8
chariots 25, 28
cheese 14
chestnuts 14
children 14, 16, 28
city-states 7, 10, 20, 24, 28
climate 14, 24
cloth 14, 18
clothes 13, 16, 18, 19

cooking 15, 16
countryside 8, 10, 14, 15, 22
craftsmen 16, 17, 20
crops 8, 14, 15, 22

D
dancing 12, 22, 24
Delphi 26
democracy 10, 11
dinner parties 12, 15, 17
Dionysus 22
doctors 26, 27

E
Egypt 8, 14

F
families 16, 17
farmers 14, 22
fields 14
fish 14
food 7, 8, 14, 15, 22, 23
fruit 14, 16
funerals 12
furniture 15, 17

G
games 24, 25
girls 16, 17, 22, 28
goats 14
goddesses 20, 21, 23
gods 20, 21, 22, 28
government 7, 10, 11

grapes 14
grapevines 14
'Greek Key' pattern 19

H
hairstyles 18, 19
health 26, 27
Hippocrates 26
honey 14, 23
houses 16, 17

J
jewelry 18, 19
juries 11

L
language 8
laws 10, 11
leather 14
lentils 14

M
make-up 18
market-place 13
mathematics 7, 26, 27
meals 12, 15, 17
meat 14
medicine 7
Mediterranean Sea 8, 14
Middle East 13
milk 14
music 12, 16, 22

O
oligarchs 10
olives 14
olive oil 14, 15, 16
Olympia 25

Olympic Games 15, 24, 25
Oracle 26, 27

P
Panathenaia 23
Parthenon 20, 21
Persians 7, 29
Phoenicia 8
plays 7, 8, 12, 13
poetry 7, 8
politics 7, 10, 11, 12, 13
priestess 22
priests 22, 23, 26, 27
Pythagoras 27

R
religion 22, 23, 27
religious festivals 12, 22, 23

S
sacrifices 22, 23
sandals 18
science 26, 27
seafood 14
servants 14, 15, 16, 18, 23
Sicily 8
singing 12, 22
slaves 12, 14, 15, 16, 17, 18
soldiers 18, 28, 29
Sparta 18, 28

spinning 14
spirits 20, 21
sports 12, 24, 25
statues 20, 23
sugar 14
symposia 15

T
temples 20, 21, 22, 23, 25, 26
theatre 12, 13
traders 8
Turkey 8, 19
tyrants 10

V
vegetables 14, 16
voting 10, 11

W
war 7, 24, 28, 29
warships 28, 29
water 15, 27
water-clock 10, 26
weapons 28, 29
weather 14, 24
weaving 14
wedding 12
wheat 14
wine 14, 15, 16, 22, 23
women 13, 14, 15, 16, 17, 22, 24, 25, 27
workshops 16

Z
Zeus 24, 25